The 4-Step Guide For Natural American English

Geoff Anderson

Audiobook & Ebook at www.fluentamerican.com

100 / ɛ/in "red"

101 /eɪ/ in "place"

Introduction

When I first started teaching pronunciation, I taught about the way that many other pronunciation teachers teach it as well.

A lot of my focus concentrated on where the tongue is, how round the lips are, how straight the lips are. In this style of teaching, a lot less focus goes to what's happening from your throat downwards. You may know what I'm talking about if you have taken linguistics courses, or if you are actually an English teacher, or help others with aspects of pronunciation.

If you have studied pronunciation for any length of time, you've seen the charts, found the visuals; you have heard these very descriptive techniques, with teachers or textbooks saying, "Oh, you need to do this, or you need to do that" with your lips or tongue.

I was doing a lot of the same because that's honestly just how I was trained. Then over time, I found I had a couple of students I was working with who had really great mouth position. Technically they were putting their tongue and lips in the right spot. There was a problem though. You would listen to them, and you could clearly tell that they were not native speakers.

That was one of my first indications that something wasn't quite right.

Another issue I ran into was that in many pronunciation videos, the teachers would tell you to do specific positions with your mouth. For instance, they may say that for an "o" sound or a "w" sound, you need to round your lips. The problem is that, sometimes even in the same

video, that same teacher would later pronounce the sound
with lip position that was completely different.

So I started to ask myself, *why is this happening?* Why
are we able to achieve a natural sound if we have round lips,
but also if our lips are straight?

What I've discovered is that, yes, mouth position can
work, but a lot of times, it also can lead us to speak in ways
that are more similar to our first language.

For instance, for the /u/ "oo" sound, a lot of
languages have something comparable, but the placement's
higher and the lips are rounded and tighter. So when students
make the /u/ sound in English, the sound isn't quite right. I
wanted to find something that could explain the difference.

This is when I started my exploration of other
concepts. Eventually, I landed on the four steps that I now
spend so much time talking about: placement, pitch, breath,
and weak consonant sounds. These, in my opinion, really
explain why you can talk with very, very exaggerated mouth
movements, but you can also talk with very minimal mouth
movements as well, and still sound natural. You may have
seen it yourself, with Americans barely moving their lips but
being completely understandable.

I have learned that in American English, we're not
focused on individual sounds. We're not focused on the 44 or
more consonant and vowel sounds that exist in American
English.

This is good news! I don't know about you, but if I
were trying to talk and remember 44 different mouth
positions, I would find that to be very difficult. I don't have
time to talk and think, "Oh, for this sound, I need to do
round my lips, but the next sound, I need to put my tongue

between my teeth." I don't have time to memorize 44 sounds and put them into practice.

I'm much more interested in what I believe are the four steps that I want you to think about every time you talk. I think it's easier to remember four things than 44.

<u>Step 1: Placement</u>

The first thing I need you to think about is your placement. Where are you projecting from when you talk? Going back to that /u/ sound, if you're projecting sound from your lips, like farther forward, very frontal, like "oo, oooo," it's going to be hard to sound very natural.

But if I make sure that when I'm speaking in English, if I'm projecting from a lower position, closer to my diaphragm/chest, there is going to be a pretty big difference sound-wise. You will feel a difference in your body; you will also learn to hear the difference yourself. So can your listener; I guarantee you. That's the very first thing: everything you say, you generally want said from a lower placement.

When learning more about placement, my first tip for you is to try to find one sound that you can make consistently with a lower placement. Maybe it's an /a/ sound like in "stop," maybe it's an /u/ like in "tooth." No matter what sound you use, it should be able to project from the same spot.

<u>Step 2: Breath</u>

The second thing I need you to consider is to consistently get airflow and breath. You always want to be able to feel your diaphragm. If you're not sure what your diaphragm is, it's an organ that's right below your chest and lungs. You need it to breathe, but a lot of English learners are not using it effectively. Instead, their lungs are doing all the work when they speak, and that creates a sound that's a lot tighter and that blocks air. It's a lot more confined. It's not as open, and it's not as resonant. American English, in general, is really looking for lots of breath, lots of resonance, and lots of bass.

If I put my hand on my stomach and breathe out, my diaphragm slowly contracts. I can feel my stomach get smaller. That's what you want when you speak in American English. Try to feel your diaphragm contract because if you don't, your words and syllables will become a little choppier, and there will not be any strong resonance in your voice. Speaking with a higher placement with less breath can still be clear and understandable, but it's not the most natural sounding. My challenge for you: if you speak in English today, I need you to be thinking *how can I engage my diaphragm as I talk? How can I keep my placement low?*

<u>Step 3: Pitch</u>

The next thing that I found to really be transformative with my students in their speech is adding a wider range of pitches. What are pitches? Consider a piano, how the left side has lower bass notes while the right side goes higher. How many of those pitches are you using in your normal life?

If you start listening to native speakers actively, you're going to find that they're probably using more pitches than you are. For instance, listen to a native speaker say the word "wow" with a lot of excitement, and try to copy them. Are you able to go as high as they do in pitch?

This is a key component of American English. We need to go high, and we need to go low, and we need to be able to hit both highs and lows often in the same sentence.

What we're also going to find is that in sentences, basically after every thought group or every group of words, we're going to change the pitch. So a sentence with three thought groups is going to have three different pitch levels potentially.

<u>Step 4: Weaken Consonants</u>

American English really doesn't care about consonant sounds. This is a concept that's easy to say but hard to implement. We're so used to speaking in a way pushes consonants! Consonants allow us to speak in a way that's clear and understandable. However, that clarity is also the issue that, in all honesty, is hurting our English the most.

Consonants block breath and flow. Also, because many consonant sounds exist across languages, we are used to pronouncing them with our first language placement. These cause immediate problems!

Remember: we are trying to open up our vowel sounds and extend breath. What often happens in American English is consonant sounds almost become vowel sounds. Listen to native speakers. We hear the "T" in a word like center completely disappearing. The L at the end of "trouble" sounds softer and lighter than the "L" at the start of "life." You can hear some native speakers say a phrase like "and then" as "an nen".

In summary: When I shifted away from focusing on individual sounds and correct mouth positions, and instead I started teaching placement, pitch, breath, and weakening consonant sounds, I was amazed by the differences in my students' speech! In fact, we find that we don't need perfect pronunciation. We don't need perfection for every individual sound. Placement, pitch, breath, and weak vowels are the tools that are going to capture the rhythm of the language in a way that sounds a lot more natural.

If you agree with me, and if you have found something similar in your own speech, I would love to hear about your experiences. Share them with others. We're trying to really transform the way pronunciation is taught.

The problem is a lot of teachers aren't even mentioning these concepts. You can see the issue in some of the most widely used pronunciation textbooks. They'll have charts of mouth position; they'll give detailed sentence descriptions of where they believe tongue should go. But there's no mention of alternatives! There's rarely any mention of placement! There's no mention of breath, or diaphragm. There's rarely a mention of pitch. The idea of weakening consonant sounds and strengthening vowels never appears on the page. With these 4 steps, we can achieve a more natural sound, often times faster.

Before we move forward, please note that a free videobook version of this guide can be found at www.youtube.com/fluentamerican. An audiobook and ebook version are available for purchase at www.fluentamerican.com These editions will make going through the exercises easier as you will be able to listen to my models.

Why English Learners Struggle With Pronunciation (13:08)

I was working with a student recently. We were practicing a schwa sound, discussing placement and pitch, and she was having difficulty. I would go up 5 times in pitch, "uh, uh, uh, uh, uh," but she would get a little stuck, repeating the same pitch over and over without any change. Though she naturally had a higher-pitched voice than me, I could consistently reach a higher pitch than her at the end of the exercise. How could I, a male with a relatively lower voice, use higher pitches than she could?

There was obviously something happening. There are times when we try to produce a sound, and we just have difficulty. Maybe we're working on a dark "l" sound, like at the end of a word like "pencil." "Pencil" does not typically end with a very firm L. However, a lot of students have not been taught about the dark "l" or they assume that an "l" makes only one sound. So even if try to say the word "pencil" with a dark L, it's easy to return to an L that feels comfortable to us.

I've spent a lot of time thinking about what's happening. The sound itself often isn't the issue because there are times in class where we can produce the sound clearly on its own. But then when we use it in new situations, or add vowels or consonants around it, we run into difficulty.

What I believe the issue to be involves psychology and fear. We have been taught to produce sounds a certain way. We've been taught that from our first language. We've been taught that from our education. We've been taught that by ourselves to a degree because as we learn a language, we have to understand we're biased.

When we learn a new language, we have to understand that we hold onto our first language. When this happens, we are preventing ourselves from taking on aspects of the second language.

It's similar to creating a soundproof wall between us and our new language. We're not even allowing ourselves to hear any alternatives.

We have this idea that a sound has to be pronounced a very specific way. An "n" sound has to sound like a specific "n," or an "l" sound has to sound like a specific "l," or a "t" sound has to sound like "t." The tongue must go here. The lips must do this.

Our first language is very different than American English. Most other languages have a much heavier emphasis on a syllable-timed rhythm. So the rhythm sounds like "D, D, D" with a very choppy, very regular sound. In addition to heavier consonant sounds, many other languages have shorter vowel sounds, and much more separated syllables that are very clearly defined.

American English is not like that. Because American English is going to require you to use softer syllables with consonants, it's going to require you to reduce portions of words to the point where they may no longer even be there at times. If you're coming from a language where that doesn't happen, or if no one has taught you this and you've studied English for 10 or 20 years, this can make you really uncomfortable.

Even if you do the exercises with me, there's still a portion of our mind that thinks, "*Wait a minute. Yeah, I hear what I'm being told, but I want to make sure that my word is clear. If I get too lazy—if I take the sound away too much—no one's going to understand me.*"

We have to understand that for a natural sound in American English, we do not want clarity. In fact, the tools that give us clarity are often the same tools that give us a heavier foreign accent.

When you are speaking super clear English, it's understandable, and that's great. It's also not the type of English that native speakers use. Native speakers use an English that's much messier. Native speakers often lack clarity. Take a phrase like, "I did not know that." Your th-sound on "that" may have been very clear, along with the d-sounds on "did". That's not how native speakers talk though. Native speakers often say something that sounds more like, "I -idn -oh —at" for "I didn't know that." It's a very different sound!

For a lot of students who struggle with concepts like placement and breath, the issue isn't that they physically struggle. Instead, there's a fear. *"Oh my gosh, if I do this, it's going to feel so weird to me. How is anyone going to understand me if I say 'din't' instead of 'didn't'? How can anyone understand that?"*

But the reality is, your listeners will understand you. In fact, they expect it. In American English, your listener is especially listening for your vowel sounds. Your consonant sounds very often can become super reduced, weak, and at times even removed, and your listener won't even know, as long as you use the right vowel sound in the right context. Your listener's mind is going to understand.

We need to trust our listener.

We've been taught that we're second language learners, and so we need to be very clear because people won't understand us. We've basically been taught that people won't understand us because we have an accent.

In reality, what we need to be taught is that your listener's brain is a powerful machine. As long as you can get a sound that's close enough to what they expect, they will understand you. It doesn't need to be perfect. Perfect is what's causing the accent.

We really want to try to focus on the actual sounds people are using. You need to trust yourself that, even if it feels very strange to you, this new approach to pronunciation will actually cause you to sound more natural. We have to trust our listener is going to understand us if we're meeting their general expectations. If we go for clarity, we're just never going to be able to achieve the natural sound you want!

How do we start? Let's begin with listening.

What I would encourage you to do is, for instance, when you're watching a show, try not to use subtitles. Or if you're listening to an audiobook, try not to look at the text. Try to treat your learning much more like how children approach language learning. When they're learning to talk, they don't know how to read. The only tool that they have is the sound. They're just listening to other people, and they're really trying to copy those sounds. When you're shadowing, try not to use the transcript. Pay attention to the sounds that they're using. Even if they don't make sense to you, try to copy those sounds.

1st Step: What Is Placement (24:06)

What is placement? What are the things you need to consider when you're doing it? How can you use it to sound more natural?

If you ever feel like you have pretty good mouth position, doing the right movements with your lips and your tongue, but still hearing an accent, one of the reasons could be that you're projecting from a different spot.

I want to show you, especially in the audiobook. Let's take a look at your first language. I need you to pronounce an /i/ sound in your first language, which can be found in a word like "sleep" in English. I need you to hold the vowel for two or three seconds.

What you may notice if you hold that for a couple seconds, you actually start to get some vibration, in your cheek area, maybe your teeth, your jaw, or your skull. Your head shakes a little bit.

That's a sign that you are using a high placement. You're projecting sound high. Note that this is not the same thing as your vocal chords. Your vocal cords are in your throat and will vibrate for vowels and some consonants. That's not the vibration for placement we're talking about. We're really talking about where you're actually projecting the sound from.

If that's still not clear, make an /i/ sound and go down in pitch five times. I'll give you an example in the audiobook. Can you hear that difference with each step down, where I'm moving the sound closer to my chest?

You might think to yourself, *"Geoff, this feels like a completely different sound."* The reason it sounds so different is because it's coming from a different spot. Every single language has its own place where it's projecting sound from. When you're studying a new language, not just English, but any language, the very first thing I would tell you to do is this. Before you study vocab, before you study grammar, before you try to talk, try to figure out where the language projects sound. If you can unlock that from the beginning, it can make your pronunciation journey much easier and faster.

American English is consistently in a lower spot for many native speakers. There are times where it goes higher, but overall, we're going to be projecting from lower positions.

As we do these exercises, keep in mind that placement is one very important step, but it is not the only important step. So if you do not have the right amount of breath and airflow, then even if your placement is good, you might end up talking in a way that does not sound natural. So it's important to continue using your diaphragm and getting enough air. Placement by itself isn't going to solve all of the problems.

Placement Exercise

Let's do a couple of quick exercises to show you how you can practice your placement. I'll demonstrate in the audiobook so you can follow along more easily there, too. Let's use the /i/ or 'e' sound again. We're going to start off with a higher placement. Maybe it's more similar to your first language. Then we're going to send it down five times until we are closer to our chest. 'E e e e e.' If that's difficult for you, you can also try dragging the sound. Say 'e' again and push it down gradually over two or three seconds. 'E.' Okay, then let's try dragging and then repeating the final sound. Let's try with an example word; let's use the word 'deep' and repeat the exercise, moving down from a higher placement to a lower placement.

This is how you can practice placement with a word you find difficult to say, or that keeps returning to a higher placement. Start with the vowel, like the /i/ in "deep", and work down to a lower placement. Then, add a consonant sound before or after that vowel sound, and repeat the exercise. So, go from /i/ to /di/.

Note that consonants are very tricky because what consonants want to do is send your placement higher. For instance, for the letter M, many English learners use a placement that is closer to their lips than their chest. This makes sense: to make an M sound, you do have to press your lips together. However, for a natural sound, press your lips together, but keep a low placement. A low placement isn't just for vowel sounds. In American English, it's also for consonant sounds. When you reach a low vibration, that's our goal. American English likes that warmth, that richness, and that resonance.

To finish studying placement with a word, add the rest of the consonants and vowels.

In a word like "deep", this means moving from /i/ to /di/ to /dip/ or "deep". Pay attention to what you find to be difficult. Maybe going from /i/ to /di/ is easy for you; maybe saying /i/ then /ip/ is harder as your placement keeps rising. This is important to understand as it lets us know what sounds we want to study more.

As you do these exercises, you will see placement works with individual vowel and consonant sounds. You'll see placement work with words. Placement is also going to impact entire sentences. So let's add to the word "deep." Our goal will be to say a whole sentence with a low placement. 'He's in a deep sleep.'

Let's do the very first placement exercise that we did, where we send placement down five times. So we're going to start high.

1. 'He's in a deep sleep.' (highest placement, concentrated around lips/mouth)
2. 'He's in a deep sleep.'
3. 'He's in a deep sleep.'
4. 'He's in a deep sleep.'
5. 'He's in a deep sleep.' (lowest placement, concentrated around the chest)

What I see with a lot of students when they do that sort of exercise, moving it down five times, is that the best sound tends to be number three or number four. Numbers one and two are too high. Number five is too low and the voice often gets a little strained. A lower placement should never be painful or cause strain, though it's fine if it feels weird or slightly uncomfortable at first.

If you're not used to placement, one of my initial goals for you would be to try to find one sound that you feel comfortable with. It might not be the /i/ sound. Maybe it's going to be the /a/ sound, like the "ah" in "stop."

Try the same lowering exercise, going down five times: 'ah, ah, ah, ah, ah.'

Or maybe it's the schwa, or 'uh' sound, like in the word "does." Try going down five times with this vowel: 'uh, uh, uh, uh, uh'.

Maybe it's going to be the /u/ or 'oo' sound, found in "tooth." Whatever sound it is, we want to have our one sound that we can use as our benchmark and as our way to regulate ourselves. If I have one sound that I feel confident in, but another sound I feel less confident in, we can use the first to our advantage.

For instance, if I feel confident with an /i/ sound, but I have trouble getting the placement right with the /u/, I can use my /i/ to help. I can hold the /i/ for a couple seconds, then transition to an /u/ without pausing. I try to note if my placement changes. My goal is to keep my placement in the same, low position for both sounds.

You can do this with any sound that you feel comfortable with. Start off with the stronger sound, and then try to alternate. You can go slow to try to catch the moment when your placement rises. Use this strategy also when you have a word with a consonant that wants to shift your placement higher. We see this a lot with the letter 'N,' the letter 'L,' the letter 'B', and 'P.' These are consonants that, if you're not careful, will send your placement higher. So, for instance, if I have the word 'seen', what you may hear is that your placement goes up on the 'N.' But I want to try to keep that placement down, even as the vowel morphs into the N sound.

Another issue that occurs with consonants is some people may add vowel sounds before them. It's like 'seen' becomes two syllables: "see" and "uhn." If you slow it down, you can begin to see where the problem is, and then you can try to smooth it out more.

Lip Position (35: 16)

I want to spend some time talking a little bit about lip position. The reason is maybe you've studied a sound in American English, for instance, like the /u/ or 'ooh' sound, 'ooh' like in 'tooth' or 'two' or 'room.' When you see a lot of teachers teaching this, one of the things you'll see is they'll tell you to round your lips. You may even listen to them and think, *"Geoff, that sounds pretty good, that sounds very natural."*

Those round positions certainly can work! However, there is a problem potentially. Some of these sounds also exist in your first language. For instance, the /u/ 'oo' sound is a pretty common sound; almost every single language in the world has an 'oo' sound. Most likely, in your first language, what happens when you make that 'oo' sound is your lips start to become pretty round. You may even feel your placement and your tension in your mouth changes.

What we find is that when we do these round positions with our lips, we start shifting back into our first language mode. We end up with a sound that is more natural to our first language. This is the danger of having these mouth positions that end up being very similar to your first language. While it is possible in American English to have those round lips, we have to be careful not to transition back to what would sound natural in our first language.

That is one of the reasons why, when I often teach a sound like the 'oo' sound, I don't typically recommend having round lips. I don't want us to get back into that mindset of our first language. I want us to treat American English like its own language, separate from your first language, not an extension of it.

How do I typically teach a vowel like /u/ then? Well, instead of doing 'ooh,' what I typically recommend doing is straightening the lips and feeling the diaphragm engage.

In general, you can get the sound equivalent whether your lips are round or straight, and it's actually going to sound great in American English. Also, I think if you're able to keep your lips straighter, it's going to be helpful in trying to keep your placement down, especially as you transition to other sound. Lastly, I think that's going to be very helpful for your mind to treat it as a new position, separate from your first language.

We see this with a couple of other sounds too. We see this, for instance, with the /oʊ/ or 'oh' sound. The way you may have seen a lot of teachers teaching an 'o' is with lips that round, especially towards the end of the vowel, which again may be similar to what you find in your first language. I personally, again, would recommend keeping straight lips throughout. You may hear some slight differences, but it's not enough for native speakers to really notice the difference, and the benefits of a lower placement and a more engaged diaphragm will have a bigger positive impact.

The reason this all works, the reason why I can have straight lips and a low placement and still maintain a pretty natural sound, is because what happens by the mouth is much less important than what's happening from your throat down. Because American English is using a low placement, American English relies much more on the tension and the control of your diaphragm and your chest. So you can have straight lips, you can have a low placement, and it's not going to affect the sound too much, as long as you're keeping the diaphragm engaged, as long as you're getting the breath support you need, and as long as you're maintaining that low placement. The whole point of this is just to be careful with the positions that you use, especially if you're studying them in a language that you're already familiar with. Try to find a way to maintain a low placement, but use positions that are different from your first language. Use sounds that are different from your first language. It might feel weird at first, but it can be very, very helpful in not shifting back into your first language mode. Check out the audiobook for more example exercises.

2nd Step: Weaken Consonants 43:02

In American English, our goal is to weaken our consonant sounds and strengthen our vowels. If our consonant sounds are not weak, there's a great chance that we may say a sentence, such as

'They didn't regularly travel back to the rocky scene,'

with noticeable issues. That's a very consonant-heavy sentence after all, with th-sounds, d-sounds, l-sounds, r-sounds. If we aren't careful, it can become very tight, with not a lot of breath coming through, a placement that is really high, and a rhythm that is honestly a little painful to say.

Our goal is to try to smooth this out. We're going to do that by trying to weaken our consonant sounds and actually treat them more as vowel sounds. I'm going to target some specific words here that can be a little bit tricky. Let's start off with 'regularly,' because I know this tends to be a word that people just hate saying. There is a chance you are going really heavy on your R sounds and your L sounds. But we have to remember if American English only had one rule, the rule would be, *'How can we keep breath flowing? How can we continue to get that airflow?'* As long as you remember that for every syllable, you'll be okay.

So, in "regularly," written in American IPA as /rɛgjələ˞li/, we need to keep the air flowing. Focus on the vowels. Let's start off with our stressed vowel. Our stressed vowel for 'regularly' is the 'e' or /ɛ/ in the first syllable. Let's then add all the other vowel sounds. So ɛ then jə then ə˞ then i. That's basically our sound; can you go from vowel to vowel? Then we can add the consonants back in. But as we add the consonants back in, we need to make sure that the vowels stay the same strength.

Try alternating between / ɛ jə ɚ i / (just vowels) and /rɛg jəl ɚ li/ (vowels and consonants) several times. The goal is to always have the vowels be stronger than consonants. Also, make sure the vowels do not change their sound at all as you alternate.

For another example, how about 'they didn't?' If you're saying 'they didn't,' you may find you're pronouncing it without any vowel sounds at all! The TH and D sounds might be taking over. That is not what we're going for.

We need to open up our vowels. So, 'they' has that '/eI/' vowel. Let's just get that vowel sounding naturally on its own. For "didn't," we have two vowel sounds actually. We have a short 'I' or /I/, which is followed by another short 'I' or unstressed schwa /ə/ sound. So the vowels in "they didn't" can sound like /eI/ + /I/ +/I/, or /eI/ + /I/ +/ ə /.

Now alternative again between vowels and the full phrase several times:

/eI I I/ and /ðeI dIdənt /

What you're going to find is that for a lot of consonant sounds, in a lot of ways, they don't matter very much. For the 'th' on 'they,' you don't need to say it very strongly. It's honestly not about the 'th.' It's about the sound after it.

Let's return to our example sentence:

'They didn't regularly travel back to the rocky scene'

Let's target the word "travel", or /tɹævəl/ for a moment. You might be used to saying this like 'travel,' with the tip or your tongue really high, touching your top tooth or alveolar ridge. I'll be honest with you. If we're treating consonants more like vowel sounds, the letter 'L' wants to become a vowel sound. You can make the 'L' into more of a vowel sound if you use a dark 'L,' so instead of saying with it with the tip or very front of your tongue making contact with the top of your mouth, take the contact away. Lower the front of your tongue to touch your bottom front teeth or the bottom of your mouth. You can even open your mouth a little wider.

Another exercise to do to weaken consonant sounds: say the word three times. Travel, Travel, Travel. If you feel like the breath ever gets blocked, that is an issue. Ideally, you can also say "travel" three times in a single second or faster. The easiest way to do this is by focusing on the vowels, or /æ/ then /əl/.

Again, try alternating: /æ əl / /tɹævəl/ /æ əl /

/tɹævəl/ /æ əl / /tɹævəl/

Let's move on to "scene". There are a couple of letters in English that really want to ruin your pronunciation, and that letter N is one of them. When you make an 'n' sound, you want to make sure it's pronounced with a low placement. You also want to make sure it's not shifting your vowel at all. In this last word, 'scene,' I often hear English learners pronounce it as two syllables, like "see" or /si/, and "uhn" or /ən/. Be sure that when saying a word that ends with N that the vowel is long enough. Don't pronounce the N until the vowel is finished, and that N is going to be very, very light.

It's time to say our entire sentence. It can be helpful to work backwards, starting with vowels then adding consonants. Try to follow this progression:

1. /a/ /i/ /i/
Rocky scene

2. /æ/ /u/ /ə/ /a/ /i/ /i/
Back to the rocky scene

3. /eI I I/
They didn't

4. /eI I I æ əl /
They didn't travel

5. /eI I I æ əl æ u ə a i i
They didn't travel back to the rocky scene.

When you try to say the sentence with just the vowel sounds, don't worry about making everything sound perfect. You might think, "*Geoff, it doesn't even make sense when I just say vowels; no one talks like that.*' But that misses the point. The point is trying to keep the breath flowing and trying to make sure that the vowels are standing out. I don't even care if you make mistakes with the vowel sounds, just focus more on the breath and getting the flow as you add consonants back in.

3rd Step: Pitch Analysis In Word Endings 51:09

Let's discuss ways to end your words to sound more natural in American English. This is the location in words where a lot of students struggle. They struggle often because their placement rises, or they may be tensing their throat. What I find to be one of the biggest issues though is they have trouble with pitch. This is because, especially if the stress comes earlier in the word, the ending is a section where you want the pitch to actually be going down and low enough. A lot of students struggle with that. They don't have enough contrast with the pitches in their words.

I want to demonstrate for you a couple of examples to consider when you're working with pitch in words. What you're going to see is that all of these words have stress on the first syllable. That means that as we go through the syllables, they're going to go down, down, down, lower and lower in pitch. The reason is simple in theory. When a syllable is stressed in English, the pitch rises slightly and the syllable is slightly slower. When a syllable is not stressed, it wants to go lower in pitch and speed up. To really understand what we're discussing, I encourage you to check the audiobook.

Our first word, *wallet*. I need the second syllable, "et", to go a little bit lower in pitch. It's also going to be very weak and very fast. Wallet. Try saying that three times. Wallet. Wallet. Wallet.

We're going to get a very similar idea with our next word as well. Bullet. You need to make sure, again, that the second syllable is low enough in pitch. Bull—higher pitch. Et—lower pitch. You may also note that these two words use a dark 'l' sound. I'm keeping the tip of my tongue down against the bottom of my mouth when I say that L.

How about our next word? Beautiful. Now we have three syllables, but the stress is still on the first syllable. The "be" sound will be higher in pitch and be held a little longer in time. The other syllables need to be said faster, with each syllable going down in pitch.

As you go through the example words, think about stress and pitch. Experiment with putting higher pitches on the wrong syllable and how unnatural it may feel. Note the change it makes in how the word sounds. Another experiment is trying to pronounce every syllable with the same pitch. Record yourself as you do it and listen to your voice. Notice how the sound will not sound natural, especially if you compare how native speakers say the same word.

To explore pitch and stress more, I want to introduce a concept called a compound noun. In a compound noun, we have two words that join together to make a single thing. A lightning bolt is a single thing, two words but one noun. Lightning bolt.

In a compound noun, we stress the first word. So in lightning bolt, I stress 'light,' giving it the highest pitch and the most time. For the other syllabls ("-ning" and "bolt") I just go lower and lower in pitch while speeding the syllables up. If you notice you have trouble making syllables lighter or weaker, you can even whisper them if you really want to. For instance, try saying "lightning bolt" while whispering "bolt."

More On Pitch Basics 55:43

Now that we have introduced pitch on a syllable level, let's apply it to sentences. The best way I can describe the concept is to consider an apartment building.

We have to understand that in American English, we have floors. When I say floors, we're going to treat them as our thought groups, which are words that go together in a sentence. To give a quick example, the sentence "I didn't know that it would rain," I may have two thought groups:

Thought group 1: I didn't know

Thought group 2: that it would rain

A thought group is similar to a floor in an apartment building. Each thought group has a ceiling and a floor. The pitches in that thought group can't go higher than the ceiling or lower than floor.
If your pitch goes too high, you're going to end up another floor! You also can't go too low because you might even end up in the basement.

When we change a thought group, we go to a different level. A new ceiling and floor means that we need to use a different range of pitches.

So, if my first thought group is "I didn't know", I might use a higher pitch range for every word it contains. When I go to my next thought group, "that it would rain", I might use a lower pitch range.

In all honesty, if you can master this concept, how you pronounce individual words becomes much less important because you're going to have the rhythm of the language. In American English, we have to move the pitches.

This is not optional. If you do not use enough pitches, people are going to say you sound flat. They're going to say you sound robotic. They're going to say you sound monotone. At worst, people are going to tell you they don't understand you. When people don't say they don't understand you or they ask you to repeat yourself, that is typically a sign that either your vowel sounds are not clear enough, or you are not using enough pitches in your speech.

To practice this, let us build a sentence together, which you'll be able to hear in the audiobook. We're going to build it in small sections. We're going to build it floor by floor. We're going to build it by thought groups.

Thought group 1: 'I didn't know.'

Try to say that with me. Say whatever is a neutral pitch for you. Let's use rising intonation on 'know' because we're actually going to have more information coming after it. 'I didn't know.'

Thought group 2: 'that it would be.'

Let's try to say this entire thought group at a lower pitch level; we want to go down a floor.

'I didn't know' = higher pitch

'that it would be' = lower pitch

Let's add a third thought group:

Thought group 3: 'such a big problem'

You may be wondering what to do with this new thought group. Should the pitch go higher or lower? It doesn't necessarily matter the direction; what matters is that you're moving floors. If I stay on the same floor the entire time, it becomes harder for your listener to understand. So experiment and see what feels better for you. Try going higher on the last thought group; try going lower.

Common Pitch Patterns 01:01:09

What are the most common pitch patterns that native speakers use? One that we're going to introduce is basically a constant downward movement, when we go from thought group to thought group and progressively move lower in pitch.

We're going to start off our exploration of this downward trend by taking a look at this sentence here:

Every time I saw it, I laughed.

This sentence has two thought groups, potentially, that are going to be separated by the comma.

Thought group 1: Every time I saw it,

Thought group 2: I laughed.

We want to treat this sentence like we always do with thought groups. When you move from one thought group to the next, we change the pitch. So if that first thought group is high, 'Every time I saw it,' my next thought group is going to either go even higher or it is going to go lower. Lower is a very common strategy and very common rhythm that you're going to find in American English.

There are a couple of other examples I want to run through with you, though they'll be easier to understand by listening to the audiobook. If you're just using the book version, practice saying each of these sentences with thought groups that get progressively lower. I separate each thought group with a /.

Example 1:

'The first time was okay,/ the second time not bad, / the last time horrible.'

Example 2:

'If you don't want to go / and you'd rather stay home, / then maybe it'd be better / if you didn't come'

Example 3:

'The good, / the bad, / the funny, / the tragic, / the incredible, / the ugly'

As you practice, if you find lowering the pitch in each thought group to be difficult, try to shift your first thought group even higher—this will give you more room to go down on the latter thought groups.

4th Step: Breath 01:05:24

What I really need you to remember is that in American English, I often tell students there's one big rule—the biggest rule in American English. If you had to summarize American English in a single word, that rule would be *breath*. Breath is what allows us to move from sound to sound, syllable to syllable, from word to word in a sentence the most smoothly.

Our goal in American English is to really try to keep that air flowing. It's why we see concepts, for instance, like a dark 'l' sound in a word like 'little,' which means the front of my tongue is down towards the bottom of my mouth. If I say 'little' with a light 'l' sound, or with the front of my tongue high, I block breath at the end.

If I say 'little' three times, 'little, little, little,' with a light L that presses the tip of my tongue against the top of my mouth, it really blocks a lot of air. But if I use a dark 'l' sound, the air opens up and is able to move a little bit more easily.

We see this with 't' sounds. For instance, in a word like 'center,' you may be pronouncing the T in the middle, which is okay. But if you listen to native speakers, you're often going to hear them removing that 't.' Compare 'center' and *"cener"* (with a silent t). Which one allows air to move faster?

This is a key concept in American language—trying to extend breath. Our biggest tool in English to aid us in moving breath is vowel sounds. Vowels allow you to move air. Consonants are constantly blocking that process. So, our goal is often to weaken consonants and to strengthen vowel sounds. If we can get the vowel moving, even if it's not perfect, even if we have issues, we can still achieve a pretty natural sound with these tools in mind.

36

Just some gentle reminders about breath and airflow. To start, posture affects your sound. For instance, if you were to say the 'ee' or /i/ sound and you were to raise your shoulders up towards your ears, you will hear the sound quality change. If you are listening to the audiobook, can you hear how my voice changed as I raised my shoulders up? The airways were constricted; I lost some resonance. That's just to demonstrate the impact that your body has on your speech, and we didn't even change our tongue or our mouth position. The only thing I did was lift my shoulders, and the sound immediately changed.

American English rewards good posture—shoulders down, and chest out a little bit. It's going to help you engage your diaphragm more. That's the second key. We need to engage our diaphragm down by our chest and stomach. When you're talking, you want to feel a little bit of tension there. So, for instance, if I take a big breath in and then release, I can feel my diaphragm slightly tensing.

Try for yourself: put your hands on your stomach and breathe out. Do you feel your stomach become firmer? Basically, when you speak in American English, you want to feel a little bit of tension in your diaphragm. You don't want it to turn into an ab workout—speaking in American English won't give you a six-pack, unfortunately—but you want to feel the muscles engaged slightly. So, if you know that you're about to talk, prepare yourself—practice breathing a little bit to engage your diaphragm.

Okay, that's if you're mid-conversation. You won't be able to do everything I tell you, but that's something you can start doing. If there's a pause in your speech, just breathe a couple of seconds and feel your diaphragm. Breathe enough to realize, *'Okay, so that's what it feels like if my diaphragm is engaging. I'm going to try to use that when I speak.'*

The next thing is that you want to identify what's causing any problem. Let's look at a sentence to demonstrate:

"I didn't get regular sleep."

There's a couple of words here that can cause some problems. We have 'sleep', and we have the word 'regular' with two 'R' sounds in addition to an 'L.' We also have 'didn't,' which has potentially some heavy consonant sounds that we want to soften. In other words, there are lots of areas here that can cause problems.

If you know you have a sentence that you're struggling with, here's an exercise that can be especially helpful right before you talk. If you're not able to do this out loud, you can try doing this mentally in your head.

Start with your vowel sounds. Let's actually just do the vowel sounds for each of these words individually, starting from the last word. For 'sleep,' your vowel sound is /i/ or 'e', sleep.

For 'regular,' you may be thinking, *'Geoff, this is a harder word. There are those 'Rs,' there's that 'L,' there's that 'g' sound. What do I do?'* It's the same thing. Start off with your vowels. So, 'regular' in terms of stress patterns, has a heavy stress followed by two weaker stresses. I have an /ɛ/ sound, I have an /u/ sound potentially, and I have an 'ER' or / ɚ /, finishing on the 'Rs' of a vowel.

Say the vowel sounds: / ɛ u ɚ /'. If that's tricky, you need to find out what's causing the issue. So, is it the /ɛ/ sound, that first syllable? Make sure, again, you're feeling your diaphragm. If that sounds okay and you're able to get the diaphragm involved, then you can add the second vowel, which is going to be a little lower in pitch, /u/, and then you have your final /ɚ/ sound.

Once you have the vowels and feel confident in how they sound, you can then add the consonant sounds. So, alternate saying:

1. /ɛ u ɚ/

2. regular

Our goal is that when we make the switch from just saying the vowel sounds to saying the full word, there's no difference. They should sound pretty much identical.

Once you have the individual words, you can move on to the sentence. In fact, we going to do all the vowels for the sentence. Bear with me because this is going to sound wild, and there's a chance no one's ever taught it to you like this before. Listen to the audiobook to hear my example.

I didn't get regular sleep.

Vowels only: aɪ ɪ ɪ ɛ ɛ u ɚr i

Add consonants back: aɪ ˈdɪdɪnt gɛt ˈrɛgjulər slip

Hopefully, what you're noticing is that if I get the vowels right and I add the consonants back in, the sound is almost the same. That's a quick technique you can do with a sentence that you know is giving you difficulty. Focus on the vowel sounds, and try to make sure that those vowel sounds are staying the same whether you're adding consonant sounds before them or after them.

One other situation that may occur is when we add too much breath, lower the placement too much, or both! This can lead to what's known as vocal fry. If you're not sure what vocal fry means, vocal fry is where you can hear popping sounds as you speak. It's just like an overly relaxed, super-low placement. If that occurs, raise the placement slightly. If that doesn't work, try to tighten the throat just a little bit. I'll be honest, vocal fry is not a situation I see very often with English learners. This is more of a phenomenon that you see in California, a state that is famous for it among native speakers. However, as a phenomenon, it is spreading around the country, especially among female native speakers.

Breath And Diaphragm 01:17:31

We've mentioned breath several times at this point. Now, let's explore it more and the body parts we need to engage, specifically our diaphragm. What exactly is our diaphragm?

Your diaphragm is located near the top of your ribs below your chest. For instance, if you take a big breath in, did you notice your stomach expand? As you breathe out, what happens? It goes back in, right?

If you practice these breaths with a hand on your stomach, hopefully you will see your hand moving in, then contracting as you exhale. That's a sign that you're using your diaphragm. We want that contraction as you breathe out.

Now, how do we make sure that this is happening when we're speaking? Here's another exercise that we can do to tell.

Take your fists, put them on your ribs on your left and right side, and press firmly. Then, breathe in and then breathe out. As you breathe with your fists pressed against your sides, you will feel your ribs going out as your lungs get big with air, and then contracting as you breathe out and your lungs empty. This is a way you can immediately test yourself to see if you are using your diaphragm.

Try doing this exercise as you say a sentence multiple times. You want to get that slow contraction inward as you talk. I'll give you an example you can hear in the audiobook, which will show you what it sounds like if you don't use your diaphragm, as well as if you do. I'm going to say the sentence 'I live in the US' five times; as you listen, watch my chest to see if my fists move, and pay attention to the quality of my voice to see if anything changes.

'I live in the US. I live in the US. I live in the US. I live in the US. I live in the US.'

For that first time, what you may have noticed was that my chest didn't really move at all—my fists stayed in the same position without ever contracting. What you may have also heard, if you were just listening to my voice, is that the sound of my voice was clear and understandable, but tight and less natural.

What happens if we actually engage our diaphragm when we do that? Let's try this again, this time engaging the diaphragm and contracting our stomach and sides.

'I live in the US. I live in the US. I live in the US. I live in the US. I live in the US.'

What you could see there was a lot more movement. The sound is also different. It started getting a bit more resonance and warmth. You could also probably hear at the end of those sentences, 'in the US,' that the air really moving without getting blocked.

This is our goal when we're speaking in American English. We want to make sure that we're getting that airflow, a consistent breath moving outward. This is how we get that resonance; you can hear that low, warm sound.

A lot of students are talking with a tight diaphragm that moves too little. A lot of students are using such a high placement that there isn't really much resonance.

Another thing you want to watch out for is that your first language may tend to close off words at the end of them, blocking breath instead of releasing it. For instance, let's say I have the word 'go.' If I want to say 'go' three times, I want to make sure that I don't stop the breath ever. There's a couple of potential issues with that. Firstly, my vowel is just not going to get enough space to breathe. Also, this will shorten the vowel too much, even though my listener will expect a longer, fuller vowel sound. To make matters worse, this can also cause that 'g' sound in 'go' to become a lot stronger. We want to do the opposite of that in so many regards. Our goal is to weaken that 'g' sound and to lengthen that 'o' sound.

For one last exercise, let's try to do a sentence with a lot of heavy consonant sounds. Our goal is to try to say this using our diaphragm and keeping air moving. In the audiobook, I'll show you what this sounds like if I don't use my diaphragm, and I'll show you what this sounds like if I do use my diaphragm.

They didn't always know all of the real answers.

If you're using the videobook, watch my chest. Watch my hands on my chest. See if there's movement. If you're using the audiobook, listen to see which one sounds smoother.

To build on that a little bit, I'm going to say a word and gradually add words while trying to keep the air flowing, trying to feel that diaphragm slowly, gently pushing air out. Don't worry about the consonant sounds; just try to get those vowels right.

Repeat after me:

Answers.

Real answers.

All of the real answers.

Know all of the real answers.

Always know all of the real answers.

Didn't always know all of the real answers.

They didn't always know all of the real answers.

How did that feel? Were you able to get the breath flowing? Did it get a little choppy? Did your placement rise anywhere? These are the same questions to ask yourself whenever you speak in English.

How fast do you need to talk when you speak in American English? I think it's a question that's a little bit misunderstood because, in reality, it's going to vary because of a concept called contrast. If you don't know what contrast is, contrast is essential in American English. It basically allows your listener to hear different parts of your sentence because you make regular changes in key areas.

We focus on contrast a lot when we talk about pitch. For instance, you do not want to say a sentence in a way where every single word, or even every syllable, uses the same pitch. We need contrast to make it easier to differentiate your words; American English in general does not like having two consecutive syllables with pitches that are too similar.

Pitch is one way that you can immediately add contrast to your speech, but there are others. Speed is another tool that can be used to add contrast. When we say sentences, there will be parts of our sentence that we want to say faster, and there will also be parts of our sentence that we want to say slower. This is going to help our listener immensely in understanding what we say.

I've given us an example sentence, which you can also hear in the audiobook:

I promise it won't happen again.

Take a moment just to think about how you would say this sentence. Don't even necessarily worry about pitch; don't even necessarily worry about speed. Let's add some context to this as well.

We can imagine that this speaker is determined. They really want to convince their listener that they're serious and being genuine.

One way you could show that emotion is by taking the word "promise" and dragging it out longer, maybe even for a full second. Another option could be to separate thought groups and go lower in pitch. In terms of speed, we could go faster on our reduced section, *"it won't happen again.*

By holding the language—by holding that word "promise"—you're allowing it to stand out more. Your listener hears that, too! They may or may not believe you, but they're detecting that you're trying to be genuine.

How about another example sentence:

If that doesn't work, then try with the hammer.

If I'm trying to use speed to make this sentence sound even more natural and to show contrast, one word that commonly gets slowed down is the word "that." This especially occurs when "that" is used as a pronoun, replacing for a larger concept. In the audiobook, you can hear I'm dragging out "that," also going a little higher in pitch, to add some emphasis.

Then we get our last part, "try with the hammer." When reduced, the words "try," "with," and "the" are said in about the same amount of time as the word "hammer". This is because stressed words, again, are held longer. Reduced words and phrases are said faster. Please note that if you speak a syllable-timed language like many Romance languages, many Asian languages, and others, the syllable-lengths will be much more balanced and regular.

In English, because we're stress-timed, we can squeeze a lot of words into a very small section of time, however. If you try to pronounce every single word and every single syllable very clearly, it's just not going to sound natural.

How would you say this sentence when playing around with speed:

We used to have enough, but then somebody ate them.

Let's give some context. Imagine the person who's talking is a little bit angry because there aren't enough anymore. They're also being a little bit passive-aggressive—maybe they know the person who caused the problem, but they don't want to name them, at least not directly.

I think there's two words here that I would play around with lengthening. I would drag out "used," and I would also drag out "ate." You can hear my example in the audiobook. There, you can also hear how fast the "but then" is said, which makes sense as this part is reduced and not stressed.

Another example sentence for practicing speed:

That was the best trip I've ever been on.

What word would you lengthen? I personally would lengthen the word "best." That would emphasize the quality of the trip—the fact it was the "best." You could also lengthen "trip" instead, as American English likes to stress the last major content word, or noun/verb/adjective/adverb.

Whatever word you choose, notice that if you just said everything at the same pace, nothing would really stand out. You can allow a word to sound more emphasized by slowing it down and giving it more time to breathe.

What Sound To Start Studying With 01:32:07

I think a very important issue when you're learning a language or you're learning a new pronunciation system is that, sometimes, you're not sure where to start.

One type of sound that can be really helpful to begin with is a sound that exists in English, but that also exists in your first language.

There are a couple of sounds that are almost universal; a couple of sounds that almost every single language has. One sound could be an /i/ or "e" sound in English. That would be the vowel sound found in words like "seat" or "these." Another example would be the /u/ or "oo" sound in American English, like in the words "soon" or "tooth." In your language, you may find you make that vowel with particularly round lips. One final sound you might want to start with would be the /a/ or "ah" sound found in "father" or "stop."

These are helpful sounds to start with because they can really help with noticing the difference in placement and also air flow across languages. We're going to begin looking at the /a/ sound in more detail specifically.

To start, how do you even make an /a/ vowel sound?

What you're going to do is have your mouth wide, and then your tongue is going to be down towards the bottom of your mouth. You want the back, the middle, and the front of your tongue all pretty low. If I say /a/, which you can see in the videobook or if you check yourself in the mirror, one of the things you notice is the back of my throat is visible. My tongue is not blocking my view. If you can't see back into your throat, then there's a chance that your tongue's a little bit too high.

One of the biggest differences between how American English uses this sound and how other languages use this sound is placement. Like I mentioned earlier, there's a tendency for other languages to have a higher placement, projecting maybe from the top of the throat and back of the mouth. If that's the case, it's going to sound more blocked off, perhaps even closer to what you find in British English.

By getting familiar with placement, hopefully you can start to hear and understand the difference between how a word like "stop" sounds in American and British English. The mouth position is identical, but the placement is completely different. So if you're projecting sound from a wrong spot, it's really hard to sound natural.

Here are some words we'll practice in the audiobook, and we also have a practice sentence as well.

We're going to say the /a/ sound, then we're going to do the voiceless consonant afterward, and then we are going to do the whole word. We'll repeat twice for each.

Wasp / cop / lock / not / rock / pop

The wasp was not on the rock.

Let's do everything one more time a little bit faster, trying to keep the air flowing because that's going to more perfectly mirror what you do when you say sentences. When you talk in sentences, you want that air continuously flowing. Therefore, we're going to try to do all this in one breath.

Wasp, wasp, wasp/Cop, cop, cop/lock, lock, lock/not, not, not/rock, rock, rock/pop, pop, pop

For our sentence, we have a couple of /a/ sounds here, which I have bolded and underlined:

The **<u>wasp</u>** was **<u>not</u> <u>on</u>** the **<u>rock</u>**.

I do want you to be careful with the word "on." That tends to be a tricky word because of the letter "N." The letter "N" can interfere with your pronunciation very, very quickly. This is because it can cause your placement to rise up (most likely, the N in your first language uses a higher placement than the N in American English). Additionally, some learners add an extra syllable before the N sound, so "on" ends up sounding like /a/ + / ən/ or "ah-uhn." One trick you may find helpful for the N: I'm pressing my tongue down against the bottom of my mouth, not the top of my mouth or alveolar ridge. This can help lower the placement and allow more air through. Moving back to the sentence, let's work backwards.

So, our last word: "rock" "rock" "rock"

Next: "not on" "not on" "not on"

Next: "was not on" "was not on" "was not on"

Next: "was not on the rock," "was not on the rock," "was not on the rock."

Last: The wasp was not on the rock/The wasp was not on the rock/The wasp was not on the rock.

A couple of other things to note here as well. "Wasp" does not rhyme with "was." Make sure you're not pronouncing both of those words with the same vowel sound; "wasp" has an /a/ or "ah" sound, whereas "was" has a schwa or "uh" sound. Another way to think of it: "wasp" rhymes with "rock"; "was" rhymes with "fun."

The other thing I want to mention too is related to that "on the rock" part. Sometimes it can be a little difficult to say "on the rock" because of the "th" at the end. What you're occasionally going to hear speakers in North America do instead is extend the "n" sound and remove the "th." So instead of saying "on the rock," you might hear "on 'nuh' rock."

One final thing is if you're saying the sentence and thinking "*Man, this doesn't sound natural at all,*" the issue may be pitch and stress related. Let's try splitting the sentence into two separate thought groups; I have split the though groups with a slash, and the stressed word is bold and underlined. To show stress, make sure the bold word is higher in pitch and held a little longer as you say it. Make sure to change the pitch level of each thought group too:

The **<u>wasp</u>** / was not on the **<u>rock</u>**

You already may be familiar with the different types of intonation patterns that exist in American English. You may already be familiar with, for instance, rising intonation, where a syllable moves from a lower pitch to a higher pitch.

You may also be aware of falling intonation, where a syllable moves from a higher pitch to a lower pitch.

In addition to that, there are wavering intonations which can consist of a fall-rise or a rise-fall. If you aren't familiar with these, you can hear my examples in the audiobook.

So, those are the different types of intonation patterns, and our goal is to use all of them in a way that sounds natural. Something that may occur as we go through these practice exercises is that we may place stress on different parts of the word. The reason is intonation carries information, such as whether our sentence is a question or a statement, or whether we are annoyed, angry, or excited. Therefore, because each sentence has a unique context based on intonation, it will also have unique word stress.

In the audiobook, you're going to hear us practice rising intonation, falling intonation, and wavering intonation with the following sentences and phrases. I encourage you to listen to see if you can hear, and copy, the differences:

Do you really think that?

Doctor's office

Are you sure?

I don't think so.

It was good.

As you practice, please note that each intonation pattern has a very distinct meaning. When used incorrectly, people can actually misinterpret what you're saying. Unfortunately, this topic is very nuanced and difficult to capture in only a few textbook exercises. It's easy as a language learner to see some of these phrases and think that they're only said a certain, specific way.

For instance, you may look at that sentence, 'Are you sure?' and think, '*Okay, verb-subject, so this is a question. It's a yes-no question, so I need rising intonation.*'

But, even as we saw during the exercises, such a simplified approach is not the case. Rising intonation, falling intonation, and wavering intonation can all be used here! However, each intonation pattern has a unique meaning. Rising intonation may make the question more neutral. Falling intonation can express skepticism. Wavering intonation may express hesitation. All of these intonation patterns can appear in sentences, including those that you may be used to pronouncing only a certain way. Shadowing exercises, where you repeat after native speakers, can help you to pay attention to different contexts and determine which pattern works best in which situation.

Let's discuss a small technique that might make your interactions with people just a little more pleasant.

An issue I often see with people who have learned English is that they are missing some of the social dynamics of pronunciation. To give an example, once I was teaching a class on clauses, and I had a student who wanted me to repeat an explanation. To express their confusion, they asked, "What?!" I knew that what they really intended was "What did you say?" or "Can you repeat that?" But the tone that they used was firm and a little bit rude.

None of this was the student's intention. They were just genuinely trying to get me to repeat a point I had explained!

When we learn a language, especially without much actual interaction with native speakers, it can be very tricky to learn a lot of the little sociolinguistic cues that make up day-to-day conversations.

With that point in mind, let's discuss how to interact with people in a way that sounds just a little friendlier, a little nicer, and a little politer, which can completely change the way people interact with us.

This can best be demonstrated by another quick example. Imagine you call a doctor's office, and the receptionist picks up the phone. The receptionist says, "Doctor's office," with a very heavy falling intonation.

There is absolutely nothing wrong with that. It can be professional; it's using the right words. The problem is that the listener may interpret it as being colder and not very

friendly. It creates a little bit of distance between the speaker
and listener. It can even convey that the speaker is not
interested in their job, or they're just trying to go home.
Maybe their shift ends at five o'clock, and it's 4:55. My phone
call frustrates them.

How can you change this interaction? Well, a lot of
this comes down to intonation.

What we repeatedly find is that in American English,
to make something sound a little friendlier, you need to
incorporate more higher pitches and rising intonation into
your speech. To give an example of this, the first example
was "doctor's office," with a falling intonation on "office."
But what if instead we use a fall-rise, or a wavering
intonation?

By using that slight rising intonation, you immediately
make things sound softer.

Let's give another example. Say your partner comes
home, and they tell you, "Hey, I have great news. I got the
promotion at work!" Your response: "Great. Good job," with
low, flat pitches and falling intonation on every word. This
manner of talking does not incorporate their emotions into
your speech. In fact, it conveys negativity on your part.
Maybe you know the new position will require a lot of travel,
so they'll be at home less. Maybe it impacts your own
schedule and you're going to have to work later at the office
or leave for the office earlier. Maybe it means less help with
the kids.

I'm not licensed to give marriage advice, but these
negative emotions are perfectly human. In fact, maybe you
need to express that frustration to your partner. What I can
advise on you is building awareness of how your tone
conveys a lot more information than you intend. We can play

with the intonation we use to sound colder or sound friendlier. If you're worried about sounding rude or distant from your listener, adding more movement to your intonation can be helpful. A common tactic involves some sort of movement that goes up, or rising intonation, at some point towards the end of your sentence. This is going to make things sound friendlier and avoid coming off as disinterested or negative if that is your intention.

Contrast With Pauses 01:53:54

A lot of English learners are saying all of their sentences at the same speed. This isn't necessarily wrong; in fact, it can be perfectly understandable. There's nothing inherently wrong with that. I have noticed an interesting situation occurring with my students though, especially when compared to native speakers.

What I often tell students is there's a good chance you actually speak faster than a lot of native speakers do. It can be a surprise! We have this idea that fluency is connected with speed, so I need to talk fast whenever I speak. In reality, fluency in American English is really more about how we join words together. Speed can be a component of that, but it's not the only one. If your goal is to sound more natural in American English, the opposite technique may actually be more effective. We need to start incorporating more pauses and slowdowns into our speech.

What I'm going to ask you to do is potentially a little scary and uncomfortable. That is because the technique is going to go against how you have normally spoken English, probably for many years.

We've been taught that native speakers don't understand us. We've been taught that we have to speak super, super clearly. We've been taught that pauses are signs that we don't have confidence, or that we don't know vocabulary. We've been taught that pausing is a negative in our speech.

In reality, a speaker who is willing to pause for a second, even two full seconds, often shows more confidence than a speaker who talks quickly. A pause is a powerful move! You are willing to actually end your speech momentarily, and trust that your listener is still going to be there for you at the end, waiting for your next word. That's confidence, right?

Pausing is a sign of great strength in language ability. So I want us to really embrace using pausing effectively. If you listen to a lot of the great speakers of our time, they pause. Probably one of the most famous examples of the last two decades is Barack Obama. Regardless of your personal opinions on Obama, he is continuously recognized as a strong public speaker. However, he has access to all of the same speaking devices that you do!

If you listen to speakers like Obama, you will find that they incorporate pauses to great effect. Listen to graduation speeches; listen to times when people are leading meetings. You will find that pauses are important. When I was a teacher, an important feature of teaching is an idea that when you ask a question, you wait 10 seconds before speaking again. So if I'm in a classroom and I ask a question, I wait 10 full seconds before I say anything else.

Are you willing to pause in your own speech? You may not need 10 seconds when you talk, but are you willing to incorporate greater pauses than you currently use now?

Let' do a quick example of this with the following sentence, which you'll be able to hear in the audiobook:

Look, if you want to go, go.

We see "look" followed by a comma, we see "if you want to go" followed by a comma, and we see "go." Let's treat each section as a thought group for this exercise. Let's imagine that after every thought group, we're going to pause. It may be helpful to add some context to this as well. Imagine your partner wants to go somewhere, and you don't want them to go. In fact, you're a little bit frustrated. It's the end of the argument, and youwant the last word.

Were I in such a situation, I would probably add some pauses:

"Look.

"if you want to go,"

"go."

In addition to these pauses, let's discuss pitch. Remember: when you change thought groups, you want to change the pitch level. In our case, let's make every thought group go a little lower in pitch. A lot of times, lower pitches are used for a more authoritative, tenser, and angrier sound. If you keep pitches higher, they sound friendlier in general.

Try that for yourself. I'm able to slow this sentence down to take 4 or 5 seconds. Are you able to?

I encourage you when copying or shadowing native speakers, don't just imitate their stresses or vowel sounds. If they talk for 5 seconds, make sure you talk for 5 seconds too!

I also want to clarify how pauses express emotion. Pauses don't have to be to show anger. They can be used to convey other feelings as well. Maybe I really want my partner to go even though I'm not physically able to. In that case, when I say "Look, if you want to go, go," I might go higher in pitch for each thought group. Instead of a falling intonation on "go", I may use a wavering fall-rise.

You can also use a pause to emphasize different words and break up your thought groups in new ways. The first thought group may end on "you" for instance if you're thinking of the right words to say or want to show some hesitation ("Look, if you...want to go, go). The fact of the matter is you can pause anywhere in the right situation.

Besides determining where to pause, I think another issue people have is knowing how to enter a pause and how to exit it. One common strategy that native speakers do is to change the pitch of the thought group after the pause. Using our model sentence, "Look" could be said in a higher pitch and be followed by a pause; "want to go" would then use a lower pitch.

Another strategy after a pause is to use repetitions. Often when a thought group ends, your next thought group can repeat the last word you said. In our model, if the first thought group ends on "if", the sentence may become "Look **if** / **if** you want to go/ go." In this case, the word "if" ends the first thought group and starts the second.

Lastly, when a thought group ends, try not to stop the breath immediately. Instead, allow the breath to continue exhaling slightly at the end of a thought group to smooth the transition into the next. You'll be able to hear examples of extended breath in the audiobook.

Regardless of which strategies you use, the key is to embrace pausing. It may feel weird and uncomfortable at first, but as you use it more, it can actually make you a stronger speaker.

Contrast With Volume 02:02:46

We've talked a lot about contrast, starting with differences in pitch as you move from one thought group to the next. Another technique we talked about was speed, where maybe some parts of your sentence you say a little faster, and then other parts you say slower. This extended into a discussion on pauses. Contrast is key because it not only helps listeners understand you better, but also gives you a more natural sound as well.

Another component I want to explore is related to volume, or how loudly or how quietly you talk in English. Many English learners, when they're talking, tend to stay at a single volume level. By itself, this is not a problem. Once you actually start listening to native speakers more, however, you may notice there's a lot more volume shifting going on. Some words are quieter, others are louder, and it doesn't always happen the way you may expect! For instance, a stressed word sometimes may actually be quieter than the reduced words around it.

As always with contrast, this is another tool to help your listener to differentiate your words more clearly, as the changes make sure your words don't blend together. Our goal is to try to increase the range of volume that we're using. In the audiobook, we're going to experiment with the following sentences, showing you what it sounds like to change the stress, speed, and volume patterns for each.

1. *How'd you **do** that? (stress on 'do')*

2. ***How'd** you do that? (stress on 'how')*

3. *Wow, **that's** incredible! (stress on 'that's')*

4. *Wow, that's **incredible**! (stress on 'incredible')*

5. *The **first** time / **wasn't** that great (stress on 'first' and 'wasn't')*

6. *The **first** time / wasn't that **great** (stress on 'first' and 'great')*

7. *We lost by **how** much (stress on 'how')*

8. *No, don't put it on the **table**. (stress on 'table')*

Reductions With Pitch 02:10:09

There's a concept with pitch that I keep finding to be particularly difficult with students.

We're very interested in stress—as we've stated, American English is a stress-timed language—but there's a little bit of a problem with stress as well! Only a small amount of words receive stress; if English is a numbers game, then more words are *not* stressed than words that are stressed.

From a pitch perspective, this means lower pitches are going to be especially important for a more natural sound in American English. If you struggle with pitch ranges, revisit our earlier section on pitch or practice with this quick exercise: take a word like "this," and say it five times, with each repetition going lower. Imagine each repetition takes a step down a staircase.

This (*first, highest pitch*)
    This
        This
           This
              This (*last, lowest pitch*)

Another exercise with pitch is to say a single word, like "wow", very slowly. Begin at a low pitch, then halfway through the word move to a higher pitch. As you finish saying "wow," send the sound back down to a lower pitch. I demonstrate the exercise more in the audiobook.

A final consideration with pitch is that in sentences, typically on the syllable just before a stressed sound, we go very low in pitch. This helps generate more contrast to separate the stressed syllable from the reduced syllables in a sentence. For instance, if I say, "I didn't **know** that," (stressing "know"), I make sure that "didn't" goes noticeably lower in pitch. All of this is to say that, in English, it's not just about going high on your stressed words. It's also about going low enough on the unstressed words, especially right before your stressed syllable in your thought group.

We're now going to explore reduced syllable patterns with individual words. For all of the words we will look at, the first syllable is not stressed, the second syllable is stressed and has a higher pitch, and the final syllables are not stressed and move down in pitch.

For example, let's look at the word "authority." We start with a low pitch ('au-'), then we go high on the stressed syllable ('-thor'), and then we go down two more times ('-i' and –'ty'). Visually, it would look like:

THOR
AU 2nd syllable/highest pitch
1st syllable
           I
           3rd syllable

                       TY
                  4th syllable/lowest pitch

That's going to be the pattern for every single word here, pitch-wise. Listen to the examples in our audiobook for the following words; note the stress for these words is always the second syllable.

Authority / Capacity / Certificate / Competitor / A Comedy / Administer / American

We need to apply these pitch principles not just to words, but sentences. It may be helpful to start by thinking about thought groups. Remember, every time you switch a thought group, you're generally going to switch your pitch level.

64

So what could our thought groups be for this sentence:

The authorities accommodated my request for the certificate

There's always flexibility; for our purposes right now, I'll separate thought groups after "request."

*The authorities accommodated my **request** / for the **certificate**.*

I'm going to stress "request," and I'm going to stress "certificate." Knowing the stresses is helpful because my pitches move down until I get to my stressed syllable. Remember that right before my stressed syllables in my stressed words ('-quest' and 'tif'), I want to even go a little lower in pitch. Listen to the audiobook to hear my examples on how to read the sentence with these stresses, thought groups, and pitches.

**Listening Strategies To Improve Pronunciation
02:17:21**

I was talking with a student a member of our
Telegram group and our small group coaching program,
Mission: English. One of the things he mentioned was that,
in a lot of my videos, there are not many subtitles. Yes, there
are graphics with words I'm targeting, but I don't typically
include words for every single thing I say. In fact, I'm
generally against word-for-word transcriptions for whole
videos.

Take a phrase like "What do you mean?'" as an
example; imaging you saw it written in the subtitles for a
movie you were watching. From the text, you may have an
idea of how you would pronounce it.

However, what happens when you actually listen to
the actor say it? What sounds do they actually make?

They might say 'What you mean?'

They might say 'Whaddya mean?'

There are a few other options, too, but the least
common option? It's probably going to be "what do you
mean," with each word pronounced clearly and perfectly.

There's a disconnect, right?

When I read text, in my head I start to think, *'Okay, I
need to say 'What do you mean?' in a very specific way.'*

But when I just listen, I have a completely different
experience. When we're listening with subtitles and captions
turned on, we think we're studying listening, but we're really
just studying reading. After watching hundreds of hours of

movies, you may even notice that you're listening hasn't improved much. You still can't even watch a show without subtitles!

By using captions and subtitles, we are not training ourselves to pay attention to what's really important, which is the sound. So, I encourage you with listening to try to avoid using any form of text as much as possible (in fact, it's one of the reasons this pronunciation book has an audio version available).

It's another reason why I really don't recommend audiobooks as listening material for students. An audiobook's original format was a book. The way people talk in a book is different than how people talk in a natural conversation!

Before you ask questions about my audiobook for this text, I have a secret for you. The audio version of this textbook was actually made first, before I wrote the book—I wanted my students to have access to real, natural spoken dialogue as much as possible, even in the text version.

I much prefer, if you're looking for materials to use that are good for listening, using interviews or your favorite shows. Listen to everyday people having normal interactions. In fact, we have a channel, www.youtube.com/fluentamericanshadowing, where you can listen to everyday people in North America having real conversations with each other. The goal is to get that real authentic language that audiobooks, news broadcasts, and Ted talks and other presentations can't really capture.

Once you have your listening material, there are three steps to consider, and they may be more challenging than they seem. However, they are going to help you progress more quickly, and will combat one of the biggest issues I see learners struggling with. One of the worst things is when I ask a student how they study listening, and they respond that they watch movies. When I ask how much of a movie they watch, they reply they watch the entire movie. That translates to two or three hours of English, which sounds great.

However, stop yourself a moment and think about all the content you missed because you didn't understand it, or the phrases the characters said that you also want to use, but never do. What if we could use movies to study better? We can!

Firstly, pick a movie or show that you're going to be comfortable with listening to two, three, four, five, ten, or even a thousand times. Now pick a short section that you like from that show or movie. A 1-minute section is often plenty! Think about all of the words and phrases the characters will use just in those sixty seconds.

The next thing you want to do involves listening. I want you to listen to the section without subtitles, or auto-generated captions like those on Youtube. If you have a transcript, ignore it. Just listen and pay attention to the pitch patterns, stress patterns, pauses, vowels, or other pronunciation features you want to target.

Finally, you're going to listen again, and this time use the subtitles.

To recap: the first time you listened, you did not use subtitles. The second time you listened, you did use subtitles. Then you're going to repeat that process, as often as you are able to. This is how you can really start improving your listening. Each time you replay the audio/video, you're going to start noticing a different aspect of the language. Maybe you'll catch a preposition you didn't notice at first. It could be that they used falling intonation where you expected rising intonation. Each fresh listen gives us a new perspective.

One of the reasons we want to stop using subtitles and text is that they trick us. The text teaches us to look for things that aren't actually there. For example, we see the letter L, and we think we need to pronounce it a specific way, like with our tongue against the top of our mouth or alveolar ridge. If we actually take a moment to listen to how native speakers talk though, we'll notice that they may not be speaking with their tongue so high, or their lips so round, or their cheeks so tense. When there is text, we start listening for things that aren't actually there, and we can actually convince ourselves that they are there.

American English Stress 02:24:08

To get a natural rhythm for our sentences in American English, we need to make sure we're using stress correctly. Before we look at entire phrases though, let's begin with a smaller concept called compound nouns.

Even if you've forgotten or never heard of a compound noun, I guarantee you've used them if you have spoken English for some time. Compound nouns are situations where two or three words join together to form a single word. It functions similarly to how many Asian languages do, where one word consists of two or three different components. An example would be a "movie theater", where "movie" is a word, "theater" is a word, and a "movie theater" is a completely new word.

When this happens in American English, we are going to stress the first word, "movie." That means it's going to have a higher pitch, and it's going to be a little bit longer time-wise than "theater," the second word. The audiobook will have examples of me saying this; please pay attention to the stresses! I also encourage you to record yourself and compare how you sound to how I sound. Many English learners are stressing the wrong syllable (e.g., "theater") without realizing it!

We can also describe compound nouns, putting an adjective before them. Let's use the phrase "new movie theater." The key pattern to remember is that the stress still needs to be on "movie." So, the pitches will look something like below. Notice that "new" and "theater" will be lower in pitch.

movie
(higher pitch)

new
(lower pitch)

theater
(lower pitch)

Let's take a look at our second phrase, 'old textbook.' Once again, we start off a little lower in pitch for 'old,' then we go higher on 'text,' then we go down again on 'book.' Old textbook.

Here are some more phrases you can practice in the audiobook; the stressed word is in bold:

broken **cell** phone / hard **math** test / renovated **doctor's** office

Let's see how this works with an example sentence:

*I found the broken **cell** phone / at the renovated **doctor's** office.*

Remember, if you don't want to sound flat or robotic or monotone in American English, you want to make sure to change your pitch for each thought group. For instance, you could have the first thought group be higher in pitch. I've bolded the words to stress for this specific example; listen to the audiobook to hear how everything would sound.

Sounds To Watch For

Now that we have covered the fundamentals for a natural sound in American English pronunciation, I want to highlight some challenges many learners encounter. Specifically, we will be looking at the most confusing vowels, consonants, and minimal pairs that students from many different languages tend to have problems with. It doesn't matter if your own first language is Germanic, Arabic, Asian, or Latin-based; these are issues that are largely universal. As always, to get the most benefit from this section, I encourage you to listen to the exercises in the audiobook.

Short I + N 02:30:22

A short "i" or /I/ sound can be found in the "i" in "bit" or "give" or "his." The very back of your tongue is down, the very front of your tongue is down, the middle of your tongue's a little high. My big tip, though, is you want your tongue to be horizontal. The sides of your tongue should feel your top teeth. It's almost like you're biting the sides of your tongue—very gently!

The short I is commonly followed by the letter N, which presents its own problems. I'm going to encourage you to try an experiment. Try to place the tip, or very front, of your tongue down against the bottom of your mouth when you make the N sound. This will help lower the placement and open up breath; normally an N sound wants to do the opposite! As always, try to project low and feel your diaphragm as you make an N sound. The N in American English does not sound exactly like it does in your first language.

We're working with a short "i" sound, and we're working with the letter "n" because this is a combination that I see students tend to have a lot of difficulty with for a couple of different reasons.

The first reason is, one, the short "i" /I/ sound by itself is a bit of a difficult sound. There's a chance that if English is not your first language, words like "sit" and "seat" are sounding very similar, when native speakers will pronounce them with two very different vowel sounds. Another possible issue could be that words like "bid" and "bed" are sounding similar; again, these are two very different vowels in American English.

Then we want to link the short I with the letter "n." So when we have an /I/ + N, it's going to sound like the preposition "in."

As we look at our example words, which you can hear in the audiobook, please note that all of our models finish with the short I + N sound at the end.

Model words

mission / measurement / action / salesman / broken / slogan / wagon

Because these are suffixes – these are, we're talking about the ends of words right now – these are also not the stressed parts of the word, which means that we want to make sure that these "in" sounds are very weak, they're very fast, and they're very low in pitch. We don't want them to get too much emphasis.

As we practice these words, you'll notice in the audio that we start with the vowels and gradually add the consonants back in. This allows us to identify where exactly any issues occur—is the vowel the problem? Is it when we put a vowel before a consonant? Does the vowel change when it is followed by a consonant? This strategy will make any issues immediately clear to us!

/I/ → -ission → mission

As you practice our model words, you'll note that there are some bonus tips for each word that I give in the audio version. Because the tips are a difficult to write down without actually hearing the words, I've decided not to include each individual suggestion here in the audiobook. That said, I do have an experiment for you to try for the

short I sound (and honestly, it works for most sounds in
American English).

Try to do say these words with the tip of your tongue,
or the very front of your tongue, pressed down against the
bottom of your mouth/against your bottom front teeth.
That's going to help lower the placement and open up breath.
The higher positions can work as well, but those lower
positions might be an advantage for you in achieving a more
natural sound.

A dark "L" sound is a little bit different than a regular "L" sound, but honestly, I believe it is actually more frequent.

You may be used to pronouncing an "L" sound with the tip or very front of your tongue making contact with the top of your mouth on your alveolar ridge, or that little bump behind your tooth.

You can certainly make an "L" sound like that. But the reality is, if you actually listen to a lot of native speakers when they're talking naturally in conversations, you will find they're not actually making that "L" sound.

What's the sound they're making then? It is actually almost a vowel sound, with lots of air passing through the tongue not blocking very much of the breath. One of the issues students have is that they have their own expectations of the sound an L should make. This dark L sound is very different from what we believe an L should be! Students often have a difficult time making the dark L at first just because of how weird it sounds or feels to them.

For that reason, I think it's helpful to start treating the L as a very unique new sound, even if your first language has an L.

Technically any L can become a dark L, though it most frequently taught for an L that appears in the middle or at the end of words. The back of the tongue is a little high and the front of your tongue is down towards your bottom front teeth, or even the bottom of your mouth.

If you have trouble getting the back of your tongue high, or are wondering, "What does that even mean to have the back of your tongue high?" here are some points of reference.

When you say an "a" or /a/ sound, like in "stop," that's the back of your tongue going down. If you look at yourself in the mirror as you make it, you'll be able to see into your throat. If your tongue is too high, that is not possible!

Conversely, when you say the "g" sound, like in "go," that's the back of your tongue going high. The dark "L" sound is going to be a little bit lower than that "g" in order to let more air pass through. Opening your jaw a little wider and will help.

One last tip: these dark "L" sounds are typically not the stressed part of the word, and often come at the end. That means we're going to go lower in pitch very often when a dark L appears. It's also going to be faster. It's going to be weaker. Do not be too balanced with your pitches or your stress emphasis. We want that last part of a word to be very fast and to be very weak if it's not stressed. So for instance, say the word "trouble." If you find that the L is too strong at the end, or even goes higher in pitch than the first syllable, try just whispering that last syllable. Try to get it even weaker. Here are all of the model words we'll review, with bonus tips, in the audiobook:

Model words

trouble / level / middle / several / bubble / trial / feel / valuable / gobble

Sounds To Watch For: Diphthongs 02:46:21

American English treats diphthongs a little bit differently than a lot of other languages do! Diphthongs are basically sounds that have two vowels joining together. What happens in a lot of languages, though, is that each one of those vowels gets pronounced very, very clearly, with the first vowel shifting into the second.

In American English, however, what we often find is that the two vowels get more compressed into a single sound. The result is a sound that involves a lot less mouth movement, and less shifting than occurs in other languages.

To demonstrate this for you, let's take a look at some very common diphthongs that you're probably already familiar with, but may be pronouncing more similarly to your first language. We want to be very careful with the ending of diphthongs because we don't want the second vowel to become too strong, we don't want the placement to suddenly rise, and we want to make sure our diaphragm is constantly engaged.

The biggest issue I see with my students is that their diphthongs become very tense at the end with a placement that goes up the throat; the pitch often follows and goes too high. Lastly, their diphthongs tend to block too much breath.

The audiobook will give you examples to follow, repeat, and compare. As you make these diphthongs, try to limit your mouth movement. Keeping your lips straight can help!

Model sounds and words

/eɪ/	/ai/	/ɔɪ/	/oʊ/	/aʊ/
Say	sigh	soy	so	sour

Sounds To Watch For: Long Vowels 02:51:18

You may have heard of 'long vowels' and 'short vowels' without really knowing what they mean. Or worse, you may think a long vowel is held longer when you say it, and a short vowel needs to be faster. The true meaning is actually much simpler than that.

A long vowel is just as long as a short vowel; long and short do not have anything to do with time. These are names given to the concepts. For instance, "foot," which has a short vowel, can take just as much time to say as "food," which has a long vowel.

Where the concept of long vowels and short vowels becomes more useful is in situations where we add the letter L. When you have a long vowel that is followed by the letter L, you need to pronounce your vowel sound, and then finish with an "ol" sound (almost like saying the word "old"). Your word will almost sound like it has two separate syllables.

This L sound should be familiar by now—it's the dark L sound we discussed earlier in the book. Remember, any L can become a dark L in the right context. However, a dark L is particularly common in the middle or at the end of words. Raise the back of your tongue higher, and lower the front of your tongue. In fact, the tip of your tongue can even touch the bottom of your mouth.

Let us look at some example words, which you'll be able to hear in the audiobook. All of our words will begin with an S sound. I'm going to say the vowel, then I'll say the vowel with the dark L, and then we'll do the whole word.

Model words
eɪ / eɪ + L / stale

aɪ / aɪ + L / style

i / ɪ + L / steel

ɔɪ / ɔɪ + L / spoil

u / u + L / spool

Let's also compare long vowel words with short vowel words that link with the letter L. Notice again how the long vowel + L sounds like it has an extra syllable with the L. Listen to the audiobook to hear me go through the examples.

Long Vowel/Short Vowel Model Words

Steal/still   Fail/fell   Fool/full

We're going to be talking about what I find with students to be the most common mistakes I encounter with students. All of these are different vowel sounds. All these are going to be minimal pairs that you want to be watching out for.

Short I vs /i/ 02:58:42

We're going to be comparing what are known as the short "i" /I/ sound and the /i/, or letter 'e' sound. A mistake I see students making is they pronounce both of these vowels the same. However, while a form of the /i/ sound found in words like "sleep" and "these" exists in nearly every language, the /I/ sound in words like "did" and "ship" is found in less than 2% of languages worldwide. Let's review some tips to consider for these vowels.

The /i/ sound in American English, though similar to your first language, is generally going to have a lower placement. If you feel you project the sound from your teeth, cheeks, lips, or top of your throat, your goal will be to lower the placement closer to your chest and to feel your diaphragm engaging. This will be true whether the /i/ is the stressed sound, such as in a word like "sleep," or if the /i/ is unstressed, like in "happy." Please be careful, as many learners reduce the /i/ when it appears at the end of the word—the /i/ should always sound the same, regardless of its position. Lastly, the letter "i" almost never makes the /i/ sound, aside from a number of foreign words like "pizza."

For the /I/ vowel, my big suggestion is to have the sides of your tongue touch your top teeth, like you're biting the sides of your tongue. It can also help to open your mouth a little wider, dropping your lower jaw. The very back of your tongue needs to be down to allow air to pass through; if you block too much breath because your tongue is too high, your vowel sound can confuse your listener, causing words like "sit" /I/ and "set" /ɛ/ to sound the same.

/I/ and /i/ Model Words

been/bean   this/these   ship/sheep

/a/ vs /^/ 03:00:57

Very often when English learners want to make a schwa /^/ sound, which is similar to the filler word "uh," they mistakenly produce an /a/ sound, found in words like "stop."

In general, the /a/ sound is the easier for students to make because it is pretty universal—almost every language has some form of an /a/ sound. The issue in American English is placement. You want to make sure you're projecting from a low enough spot towards your chest, and your diaphragm is engaging. Other mouth position tips for /a/ include opening your mouth wider and keeping your tongue down—you should be able to see back into your throat if you make this sound while looking into a mirror.

For the schwa sound, it helps to put our face into a neutral position. There are a few body cues to know if you are making the correct adjustments. Your lips should be straight and not tensed into a smile or frown. Your top teeth and bottom teeth do not touch. Lastly, the middle of your tongue will rise, but not touch the top of your mouth. Once in this position, open your lips slightly and project low from your diaphragm. Again, this will sound like vowel in the filler word "uh" or "um."

Let's review our model words, with examples given with more detail in the audiobook.

/a/ and /^/ Model Words

Shot/shut   **lock/luck**   **bog/bug**   **not/nut**

Many learners of American English say words like "foot" and "food" with the same vowels. This is a problem, though, because despite having similar mouth positions, these are two completely different sounds!

Let's start off with the /ʊ/ sound. There are not many words that have the /ʊ/ vowel; however, the words that have it are very common. It's the vowel found in words like "look," "book," "good," and modal verbs like "could." The back of your tongue is high, the front of your tongue is down, and your lips will be straight. It may help to lower your lower jaw, or open your mouth wider.

What makes this sound more complicated is that it is sometimes followed by a dark L, like in "pull" and "full." In those situations, it can be helpful to slightly close the mouth at the end of the vowel, though it is not necessary to do this. You will hear examples of /ʊ/ followed by a dark L in the audiobook.

For the /u/ vowel, like in "who" and "room," you may find it is similar to the /u/ sound in your first language, as this is one of the most universal vowels. However, most likely in your first language, you will round your lips more to produce it, the breath will be more restricted through the throat, and the placement will be more in the mouth. American English, as always, will require a lower placement with a more engaged diaphragm. Additionally, your lips do not need to be very round—in fact, many of my students have an easier time producing the vowel when they have straight lips. Using straight lips may help you create more separation between this vowel sound in American English and the equivalent sound in your first language.

Aside from these differences, to make this sound, it will be helpful to have the back of your tongue high and the front of your tongue down near your bottom front teeth. You can close your mouth more for the /u/ sound compared to the /ʊ/ sound.

/ʊ/ and /u/ Model Words

pull/pool   **full/fool**   **goods/goose**

"Send" and "sand" have different vowels sounds. So do "head" and "had." What exactly causes the difference?

Let's begin by looking at the /ɛ/ sound, which is found in "bed" and "less," but that also comes before a lot of letters! Say F, and M, the /ɛ/ is that vowel you hear before the actual consonant. The /ɛ/ is a contradictory in many respects. As we engage our diaphragm and use a low placement, we don't want a lot of air moving through our mouth. So what we're going to do is raise the back, the middle, and the front of our tongue higher. To achieve this, it can help to close the mouth more. However, we're going to keep our airways open through our throat and chest areas. The last tip that may help is that we want our tongue to be horizontal; it can even make contact with our top teeth on the sides of our mouth.

The /ae/ sound, like in "cat" and "man," will be more open in the mouth. You can slightly smile as you open your mouth wider to keep your lips tenser. If you look at yourself in the mirror as you make the /ae/ sound, the middle of your tongue is going to go higher, while the back and the front of your tongue go down. You should not be able to see into your throat; the middle of your tongue is too high. This /ae/ sound is fairly unique to American English; most other languages do not have a similar sound. Other variations of English, like British English, will go noticeably higher in placement, if they even use the vowel.

/ɛ/ and /ae/ Model Words

bed/bad rest/rash head/had mess/mass Texas/taxes

/ʊ/ vs /ʌ/ 03:12:12

We return to the /ʊ/ sound of "book," as well as the schwa sound of "buck" because many American English learners confuse the two. There are some fundamental mouth position differences that can help distinguish them.

Remember for a word like "book" or "good" that has the /ʊ/ vowel, the back of your tongue is high, the front of your tongue is down, and your lips will be straight. It may help to lower your lower jaw, or open your mouth wider. Air will be more blocked as it enters the mouth than for schwas.

To make the /ʌ/ sound, a couple of key things will be helpful: we want to relax our jaw—remember, we want to put our face into a neutral position, not smiling or frowning. The goal is minimize tension in the jaw and cheeks. You can tell if you're relaxing your jaw if your top teeth and your bottom teeth don't touch. You're also going to notice that the middle of your tongue is going to kind of rise up, but not actually touch the top of your mouth. The very back of your tongue will be down, allowing more air to pass through than for the /ʊ/. As always for both of our vowel sound, we're trying to project from a low placement, with lots of breath coming through the chest and throat. Let's look at minimal pairs for these vowel sounds; listen to more details in the audiobook.

/ʊ/ vs /ʌ/ Model Words

book/buck   should/shuck   hood/hut

cook/cup   look/luck   good/gut

I have mentioned dark L sounds several times throughout this book because of how significant a role it has in producing a natural American English accent. The final comparison exercise I'd like to do returns to the dark L that links with an /oʊ/ sound, found in words like "old," and "coal." To make sure we begin to notice the difference between very confusing sounds, we will be looking at a schwa sound, a regular /oʊ/ sound, and an /oʊL/ sound.

A reminder that to make the /^/ sound, found in words like "fun" and "does," a couple of key things will be helpful. We want to relax our jaw. We want to put our face into a neutral position, not smiling or frowning. The goal is minimize tension in the jaw and cheeks. You can tell if you're relaxing your jaw if your top teeth and your bottom teeth don't touch. You're also going to notice that the middle of your tongue is going to kind of rise up, but not actually touch the top of your mouth. The very back of your tongue will be down, allowing more air to pass through.

The /oʊ/ sound in words like "go" and "coat" is a diphthong, which means we are taking two sounds and blending them together in the case of American English. Start with your mouth a little open, the back of your tongue high, and front of your tongue down. Towards the end of the vowel, you can close your mouth slightly, which can raise the front of your tongue. Don't exaggerate this movement, however, as it can cause your placement to rise—this is one of the differences between American English and your first language if it also has an /oʊ/ sound. American English keeps the placement down and diaphragm engaged.

When the /oʊ/ sound is followed by a dark L, one key difference you may feel is that the back of the tongue will go even higher and the mouth may close more. Do not completely block the breath though because we do not want the sound to become overly tense. Air should always be able to move easily through the mouth. As you get to the dark L at the end of the vowel, you want the sound to be fast, weak, and potentially with the tip of your tongue down (though it's not necessary). The dark L will also generally use a lower pitch.

/^/ and /oʊL/ and /oʊ/ Model Words

rubble/roll/row   **double/dole/doe**

shovel/shoal/show   **bubble/bowl/bow**

Most Common American English Vowels

To conclude our 4-Step American English textbook, let us review the most frequently used vowel sounds in American English, providing you notes with mouth position tips, spelling rules, word pairs, and example sentences. Listen to the audiobook to hear me go through each of the sounds.

/i/ in "deep"

Tips

Your mouth does not need to be very open. The front of your tongue can be down. The key is the mid-back of your tongue; it tends to be high, almost touching the top of your mouth.

Example Words and Spelling Patterns

"feet" "sleep"

"receive" "thief"

"Japanese" "evening"

"critique" "technique"

"beach" "leave"

"busy" "history"

Word Pairs

sweet dreams/ keep clean/ busy beach/

critique techniques/ happy feet/ these evenings

Practice Sentences

The **bees keep** their **honey clean** while **we eat.**

They will **critique** our **techniques** this **evening** on the **beach.**

The **study** of **history** makes **me** fall **asleep.**

/I/ in "this"

Tips

Your mouth does not need to be very open. The front of your tongue can be down. The middle of your tongue is raised. The back of your tongue is down. The sides of your tongue touch your top teeth.

Example Words and Spelling Patterns

"miss" "bit"

"quiz" "build"

"system" "bicycle"

Word Pairs

bit thin/ quick hit/ missed quiz/

this bicycle/ hit the gym

Practice Sentences

I **missed this quiz** when my **kids** were **sick**.

His trip to Italy was **finished this winter**.

Is the **gym in this city pretty big?**

/a/ in "stop"

Tips

Your mouth can be open wide. Keep tongue down.

Example Words and Spelling Patterns

"mop" "box"

"wasp" "father"

Word Pairs

father's watch/ hot pot/ stop watching/

not modern/ office job/ job offer/ doctor's office

Practice Sentences

The **doctor's office** I **stopped** at was **locked**.

There's a **rock** in my **sock** and **water** in my **watch**.

The **pot on top** of the **box** is **hot**.

/^/ in "fun"

<u>Tips</u>

Put your face into a neutral position, not smiling or frowning. The goal is minimize tension in the jaw and cheeks. Your top teeth and your bottom teeth don't touch. The middle of your tongue is going to rise up, but not actually touch the top of your mouth. The very back of your tongue will be down, allowing more air to pass through.

<u>Example Words and Spelling Patterns</u>

"dump" "bust"

"one" "month"

"young" "enough"

<u>Word Pairs</u>

one month/ young country/ loved son/

fun enough/ lump sum/ dumb luck

<u>Practice Sentences</u>

One month in **the young country** is **enough.**

We **loved the lump sum of money** we **won.**

My **son's cousin jumped up** when he **was done.**

/oʊ/ in "slow"

Tips

Start with your mouth a little open, the back of your tongue high, and front of your tongue down. Towards the end of the vowel, you can close your mouth slightly, which can raise the front of your tongue. Don't exaggerate this movement, however, as it can cause your placement to rise.

Example Words and Spelling Patterns

"ghost" "so"

"low" "blow"

"coast" "loan"

"though" "dough"

"road" "coat"

"note" "rope"

Word Pairs

go home/ low blow/ open window/ own loan/

cold dough/ slow toad/ row the boat

Practice Sentences

The **slow toad** is trying to **go home** across the **road**.

Don't smoke if you **don't open** the **window**.

The **ghost** was **clothed** in a **rose** colored **coat**.

/ɔ/ in "law"

Tips

Have your mouth open wide, but the back of your tongue high.

Example Words and Spelling Patterns

"paw" "dawn"

"talk" "already"

"audience" "August"

"boss" "solve"

"thought" "daughter"

Word Pairs

daughter's boss/ small ball/ always talk/

gone off/ thought wrong/ saw it all

Practice Sentences

The **author** received a **long applause** from the **audience**.

The **dog** we **lost** in **August walked** home by the **fall**.

I **saw** you **watered** the **lawn** and **bought** paint for the **wall**.

/ʊ/ in "good"

Tips

Keep your lips straight and the mouth a little open. The back of your tongue will be high and the front of your tongue down.

Example Words and Spelling Patterns

"book" "good"

"could" "would"

"put" "cushion"

Word Pairs

good neighborhood/ should put/ look for sugar/

cook book/ wooden hook

Practice Sentences

Look at the **book** my brother **took.**

The **cushion** on the **hook** is **full** of **wool.**

I **pulled** out a **good** picture of the **neighborhood.**

/u/ in "food"

<u>**Tips**</u>

Your lips do not have to be round, though they can be if your placement stays low and your diaphragm stays engaged. The back of your tongue is high and the front of your tongue is down. Your mouth can be slightly closed.

<u>**Example Words and Spelling Patterns**</u>

"tooth" "boot"

"whose" "two"

"clue" "statue"

"news" "flew"

"tube" "pollute"

<u>**Word Pairs**</u>

new clue/ who's new/ duke's boot/ loose a tooth/ threw out food/ news flew

<u>**Practice Sentences**</u>

I **threw** the **school's food into** the **room.**

News flew when he **threw** the **duke's boot.**

She **chooses** to drink **fruit juice** with a **soup spoon.**

/ae/ in "has"

Tips

Open your mouth wide and tense your lips slightly in a horizontal direction. The back of your tongue and the front of your tongue are down. The middle of your tongue rises.

Example Words and Spelling Patterns

"past" "man"

Word Pairs

fast answer/ past fashion/ black cat/ bad apple/

fat chance/ can't act/ at bat/ last package

Practice Sentences

The **black cat** was too **fast** to **catch**.

The **last package** was **at** the **back** door.

There's a **fat chance** the **man** has a **backpack**.

/ ɛ/ in "red"

Tips

The back, middle, and front of the tongue all will be slightly high, blocking breath in the mouth area. The throat will remain open, however. The mouth can be mostly closed; the tongue can be very horizontal with the sides of the tongue touching the top teeth.

Example Words and Spelling Patterns

"less" "best"

"measurement" "dead"

"X" "S" "F" "M"

Word Pairs

well fed/ get rest/ red pen/ better led/

best measurement/ heavy head/ never spent/

Practice Sentences

The **men** who **read** the book **said** it was **excellent**.

To **get better**, stay **well fed** and **rest** in **bed**.

Experts edited the **essays** in **red pen**.

/eɪ/ in "place"

Tips

The back of the tongue is low while the mid-front of the tongue goes higher. Your mouth can be open, though if the sound is difficult, it can be helpful to close the mouth more.

Example Words and Spelling Patterns

"hate" "safe"

"Spain" "claim"

"alien" "April"

"Friday" "May"

"disobey" "prey"

"neighborhood" "eight"

Word Pairs

hate bathing/ freight train/ April eighth/ rainy day/ safe neighborhood/ came late

Practice Sentences

The **freight train came eight** hours **late.**

I **hated** how **April eighth** was a **rainy day.**

They may get **away** to **Spain** if someone **pays.**

About the Author

Geoff Anderson founded Fluent American, www.fluentamerican.com, and all of its resources with the intention of helping English learners who want to sound as natural as possible. His 4-step approach, focusing on placement, breath, pitch, and weak consonants, has helped thousands of students with their pronunciation around the world. Before founding his own English company, he served as an instructor, an academic director at a language center, and an IELTS examiner for the speaking and writing exams. He currently lives in Ohio in the United States.